Elsie Benthien

Chehalis

ELEMENTS OF COSTUME DESIGN

*Portrait Painting by Sir Joshua Reynolds
Distinguished for Beauty and
Grace of Costume*

Elements of Costume Design

for

High School Students

MARIE DOWNS
and
FLORENCE O'LEARY

Illustrated by
LOUISE SARRAZIN

BRUCE-MILWAUKEE

THE BRUCE PUBLISHING COMPANY
Milwaukee, Wisconsin

TABLE OF CONTENTS

LIST OF ILLUSTRATIONS

PREFACE

I N presenting this book to teachers and students of clothing and design, the authors hope to interest the American girl in the selection of sane and artistic clothes.

The book is the result of the growth of home economics in the public schools, and the detailed development of the subjects relating to clothing, food and shelter. Modern public school courses are now including costume design lessons from the first grade to the eighth. This gives the teachers of sewing, who have been emphasizing elementary sewing and technique in dressmaking, opportunity to apply design to clothing.

There is a prevalent idea that art is so much a matter of feeling and appreciation, that it is difficult to arrive at a definite line of procedure which will tend to develop in the high school girl, appreciation, interest, judgment and creative power.

The material presented in this book has been used with high school students in a two-year course in clothing in which the lessons included sewing, design and textiles as regular work. The course was planned so that the design for the garment was made before the sewing was attempted, and was correlated with textile study so that the design had a direct relation to the article to be made.

For teachers who have had limited training in art and for those who received training before design was considered a vital part of the courses in sewing, this book will be found especially helpful.

In using the book, it will be found that the exercises at the close of each chapter may be enlarged upon and much collaborated material supplemented. Modern fashion books, advertisements from magazines, Japanese prints, flowers, trees, landscapes, beautiful textiles, embroideries, rugs and pictures all help to add interest.

In addition to being helpful to teachers, it is also intended that the book be of interest to sales people. The great wave of education for store service has brought the realization that in order to be efficient one should have a knowledge when selling ready-to-wear, not only of psychology, but also of textiles, design, color, line and proportion as applied to the human figure.

The authors hope that the selection of material here may, by interesting the American girl in the selection of individual clothes, be of some value in the development of American fashion.

ELEMENTS OF COSTUME DESIGN

CHAPTER I

PROPORTIONS OF THE HUMAN FIGURE

THE Greeks taught that the human figure represented the most beautiful of all divisions of space. They used eight heads as the standard of height. The French prefer a smaller figure. Some of the modern illustrators use nine heads.

In order that the proportions of the human figure may be studied, the following measurements are given for the convenience of the pupils. In measuring, the least difficult method is to let one inch equal one head.

The lengths used for the figure are as follows:

Entire length, eight heads.

One head to chin.

One and one-fourth heads to base of collar.

One and one-half heads to the shoulder.

Two heads to the bust.

Three heads to the waist.

Four heads to the hips.

The widths of the figure are as follows:

Collar, one-half head at chin.

Collar, one-half head at base.

Shoulder, two heads.

Bust, one and one-half heads.

Waist, one head.

Hips, one and one-half heads.

Bottom of skirt, two heads (standard).

Arms, one-half head wide.

The measurements from the shoulder to the elbow and from the elbow to the wrists are of equal lengths.

[13]

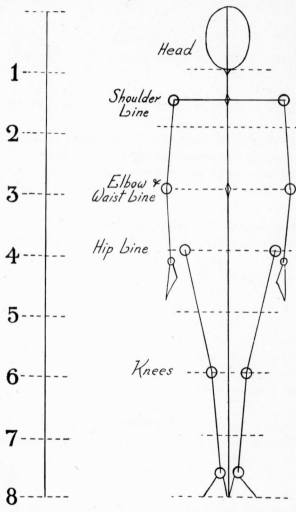

1

2

3

4

5

6

7

8

Head

Shoulder
Line

Elbow &
Waist Line

Hip Line

Knees

First Step to Proportions

If the measurements given are carefully laid out, the drawing cannot fail to give satisfaction, and you will have the pleasure of retaining the proportions drawn for future use.

Exercise 1

Choose a sheet of drawing paper 9 x 12 inches.

Through the center of the page draw a line 8 inches long.

Place dots 1 inch apart along the line and draw horizontal lines through these dots.

At the end of each line, to the right of the drawing, place numbers from one to eight.

Line one represents the base of the neck.

Line four represents what we shall call, for convenience, the hip line.

Line six represents the knee line.

The neck line is one-third distant from line one to line two.

The shoulder line is two-thirds of the distance from line one to line two.

The waist line is line three.

The same line is used for the elbow line that is used for the waist line.

The finger tips do not quite touch line five.

The ankle line is two-thirds down from line seven.

The feet should rest on line eight.

Exercise 2

In order to complete the drawing just made, draw an oval to represent the head.

Draw the shoulder line ⅞-inch on each side of the center line.

Draw the hip line ¾-inch on each side of the center line.

Put in the other lines necessary to complete the figure.

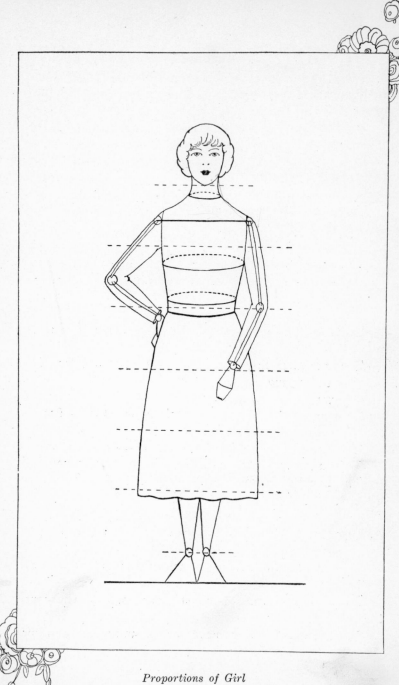

Proportions of Girl

Exercise 3

We shall not give the facial lines in this lesson, but we shall connect all the lines necessary for completing the figure made in Exercise 2.

In this exercise, the lines with which to deal are the neck, bust and waist lines.

In the "front figure" these lines curve upward. In the "back figure," the lines curve downward. The centers of these lines are higher in the back than in the front.

Complete the drawing by sketching in the waist, skirt and sleeves.

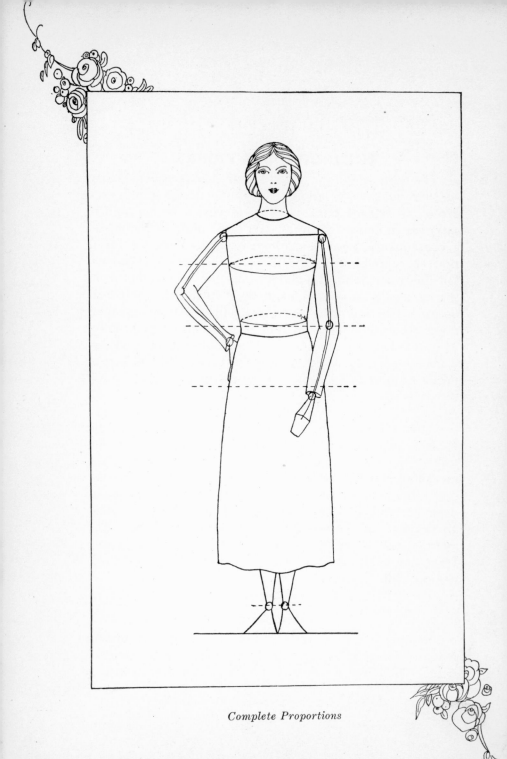

Complete Proportions

CHAPTER II

THE INDIVIDUAL FIGURE

The high school girl should study her own personality so thoroughly in relation to costume design that every dress will have a tendency to add charm to her figure, rather than detract from it. Her style of dress should, as a consequence, become distinctive. This does not mean that she should disregard the tendency of the fashions. On the other hand, she should take the best points from the modern fashions and adapt them to suit the individual figure. The following exercises will assist in revealing more accurately the lines and proportions of her figure. They will help the pupil to see if she looks better in a long-waisted dress, or in a short-waisted dress, and will be the means of more artistic planning in costume design.

Exercise 4

After the pupil has drawn the human figure from the measurements given, and is satisfied with the result obtained, the list should be considered again. Where the measurements for the lengths and widths of the figure are given, the pupil should substitute her own individual measurements and work out a drawing of the individual figure. In drawing this figure, let 1 inch equal one head. The average school figure is seven and one-half heads tall. Have one pupil take another's measure, accurately following the table given.

TRACING
Exercise 5

Tracing avoids the difficult task of drawing the human figure. The work in costume design must always be up to date. Therefore, we must follow the lines of fashion to a

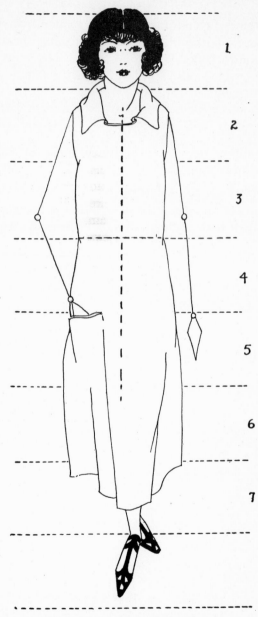

1

2

3

4

5

6

7

Skeleton Figure of High School Girl

certain extent. Selections should be guided by art principles. Choose a figure from a current fashion sheet as near
in proportion to your own figure as possible. Cut out the
figure. Then trace the outline on white drawing paper.
Make six tracings of the same figure. Keep the tracings
for dress designs and color schemes to be made later.

Exercise 6

Plan a simple dress for the figure made in Exercise 3
of the previous chapter.

Exercise 7

Plan a dress, and draw the design on the tracing of your
own individual measurements made in Exercise 4.

Morning Dress

CHAPTER III

APPROPRIATENESS OF COSTUME
THE MORNING DRESS

A dress should not only be appropriate to the wearer, to the season, and to the occasion on which it is to be worn, but also to the time of day. For the school problem, consider the three types of dresses, the morning or school dress, the afternoon dress, and the evening or party dress.

The morning or school dress, regardless of the style, should be extremely simple and conservative. The frock must be useful as well as beautiful. The collar and cuffs should be relied upon in most cases to give the dress distinction. The sleeve should be plain and moderate. The waist should be full, and above all things, comfortable. The skirt should be moderately short, with enough fullness to allow freedom of movement. Color plays an important part in the effectiveness of the school dress, and it will be necessary to refer to the chapter on color, before selecting color schemes.

Exercise 8

On a sheet of drawing paper 9 x 12 inches, trace the outline of the individual figure. Design a school dress to be made of woolen material.

Design a school dress to be made of linen or cotton material.

THE AFTERNOON DRESS

In planning the afternoon dress, the pupil will first consider the material, which may be softer in texture than that of the morning dress. The color, too, may be a trifle more pronounced, and the trimming more elaborate, but at the same time the fact should be kept in mind that simplicity is the keynote of beauty in dress design. The afternoon

[23]

Afternoon Dress

dress will vary in style according to the different seasons of the year. The materials suggested for summer gowns are those which lend themselves more easily to daintiness and freshness, and are as follows: voile, organdy, pongee, silk crepe. For winter dresses, the following materials are suggested: serge, taffeta and velvet.

Exercise 9
Design an afternoon dress to be made of thin material.

Exercise 10
Design an afternoon dress suitable for winter wear.

THE EVENING OR PARTY DRESS

A famous French authority on dress says, "No gown is an evening dress, unless it has low neck and short sleeves." Clinging materials are best suited for evening dress. In a party gown, rhythm of line, rather than rhythm of mass or spots of color, should be considered. Color plays a most important part in the selection of an evening dress, and for this reason the color of the hair rather than the eyes, should give the keynote for choice of color in the material to be chosen. A young girl should remember that even on a party gown, brilliant ornaments are to be avoided. The dress should rely upon beauty of line to give it distinction. While jet and spangled trimmings are not out of place for those of more mature years, they are inappropriate for the school girl.

Exercise 11
Plan an evening dress of soft material suitable for your own type. Make a second design for a girl of opposite type.

FASHIONABLE AND ARTISTIC DRESS

Distinction should be made between fashionable and artistic dress. Artistic dress depends upon beauty of line and harmony of color and appropriateness for its effectiveness. Fashionable dress depends upon the swing of the

Evening Dress

times, upon the prevailing color, upon the newest materials, regardless of the fact of suitability to the wearer.

A dress may be fashionable and still be artistic. This fact is often demonstrated in our modern styles. Short skirts may be fashionable, but if worn by a very stout girl, become extremely inartistic. Dull red may be the fashionable color, but if a dull red dress is worn by a girl with auburn hair, the effect produced is far from artistic.

One of the most ridiculous styles was that of the fur-top shoe, popular at a time when the skirts were worn very short. The hem of the skirt and the fur formed two awkward horizontal lines and cut the figure in such a way as to destroy all beauty.

This does not mean that the high school girl should avoid following suggestions of fashionable dress, but that she should use these suggestions with caution and emphasis upon the effect the style may have upon her own individual figure.

Exercise 12

From a current fashion magazine, choose four costumes which represent to you the newest ideas in costume design.

(a) In what way have these styles changed from the designs of last year?

(b) In what part of the costume is the change most noticeable?

(c) Are any parts of the costumes chosen unsuitable to your own figure? Why?

Vertical Lines Add Height

CHAPTER IV

SUITABILITY

On the subject of suitability of line to figure, we are not concerned so much with the normal figure, which may assume any silhouette of fashion, but principally with the tall, slender figure and the other extreme, the short, stout figure.

The tall slender girl should choose points from the fashions which tend to give breadth to the figure. On the other hand, the stout girl should avoid ruffles, broad shoulder effects, broad belts, and lines that exaggerate the horizontal lines.

In order that these ideas may be brought before you, it will be necessary to study the two extreme figures just mentioned.

Lines which go to make up a costume are generally horizontal or vertical. Lines may be formed in many ways. By braids, tucks and heavy stitching this effect is more commonly produced. We learn from observation that vertical lines add apparent height to the figure and that horizontal lines add apparent breadth.

The following points are given for convenience in planning suitable costumes:

1. Belts and girdles should be carefully considered as to width.

2. Length of coats is important.

3. Sleeves should be trimmed or broken above or below the half-way point.

4. The Greek law is to avoid one-half or one-third, in any division of the figure.

5. A ruffle, yoke, or coat must be between one-half and one-third, in order to follow the law of proportion.

Horizontal Lines Add Breadth

6. Never repeat the length of a head in a yoke or trimming on a waist. When the trimming on a waist appears awkward, it is usually because this law has been violated.

Exercise 13

Principles are often more clearly impressed upon the mind if one can be led to see the humorous side of a problem. For this reason, it is sometimes profitable to illustrate the various points by humorous drawings. Make over a traced silhouette so that it will represent a figure of exaggerated height. Add all the lines needed to make the figure grotesque in appearance, as long as the vertical lines are the ones taken into consideration.

Exercise 14

Cut out two figures exactly the same size from oak tag. Take a piece of finely striped material and place it under the oak tag. Trace it, cut out the material on the outlines, paste it to the figure, and mount. On the second figure, turn the stripes horizontally, and paste. Indicate the belt on each figure. Under the first one print the words, "Vertical lines add height," and under the second figure print, "Horizontal lines add breadth."

Silhouette

CHAPTER V

THE SILHOUETTE

The silhouette is a profile, or shadow, filled in with dark color. This idea was introduced by the ancients. Many examples of the type are found among the designs made by the Egyptians.

The making of silhouettes is of special value in costume design for illustrating good and bad division of space. Through silhouettes one may be led to see the effect of the long and short waists, also the effect of ruffles and flounces upon the outline of the figure.

A silhouette of one's own head on squared paper is of special value in showing styles of hair arrangement. It is also an effective way of illustrating types of hats that may or may not be worn with particular profiles.

Exercise 15

Design a gown in silhouette for a slender figure and mount on a light gray background.

Exercise 16

Plan a gray gown for a stout figure and mount on a light gray background.

Balance in Design

CHAPTER VI

ART PRINCIPLES APPLIED TO COSTUME

Before attempting actual work in costume planning, it will be necessary to understand the principles which underlie all forms of design. The first of these principles is "balance."

BALANCE

By the term, "balance" in design, we mean the equalization of forces. The drawing must be planned so that a one-sided, top-heavy appearance is avoided. If one side of the design is emphasized too much, the equilibrium of the whole is destroyed.

RHYTHM

Rhythm is related movement. There is rhythm in a field of blowing grain, and rhythm in the flight of birds. In planning designs, the pupil will learn that this principle of design is governed by spacing.

HARMONY

Harmony is the restful adaptation of parts to one another, and may involve both rhythm and balance. When we think of harmony, we think of relations.

Exercise 17

From a current fashion sheet, select a dress illustrating the principle of balance in design. Mount on a suitable background.

Exercise 18

From a fashion plate, select a dress showing rhythm of line. Cut out the figure and mount on a suitable background.

Dress Showing Repetition

CHAPTER VII

LINE APPLIED TO COSTUME
REPETITION

An interesting principle in costume design is the one of repetition illustrated by repeating groups of lines in various parts of the costume. For example, the same design in the waist may be carried out in the skirt. The design will necessarily vary in size. Minor changes in the design itself are also permissible, and often add a pleasing effect. Care must be taken to add enough variety in the placing of the design to avoid monotony. Repetition may be gained by using tucks, folds, ruffles, ribbon or beads.

Exercise 19

From a recent fashion sheet, select two dresses that illustrate the principle of repetition, and mount the designs on drawing paper. Make a list of the various devices used to gain the effect desired.

Exercise 20

Design a woolen dress so that it will represent the principle of repetition. Use very narrow braid as trimming.

Exercise 21

For an illustration of violation of principles, choose a dress poor in design and lacking in harmony of line. Cut out the figure and mount on a suitable background.

*Portrait of the Infanta by Velasquez, Showing the Influence of
Costume in Spain During the Early Part
of the Seventeenth Century*

CHAPTER VIII

LINE APPLIED TO COSTUME
TRANSITION

When designing a dress, use as few lines as possible. In order to produce unity and harmony, there should be but one theme expressed. When the lines conform to the lines of the figure and seem to grow out of the lines of the figure, we call this theme "transition." When lines of transition are chosen, all angles and sharp turns are avoided, and curves are emphasized instead. When lines of transition are used, they should be used to the exclusion of all other lines.

Exercise 22

Look through a fashion magazine for a gown showing lines of transition. Mount the design on a suitable background.

Exercise 23

Choose from a fashion sheet a dress whose lines fail to produce harmony. Change the gown to represent a theme of transition.

OPPOSITION

Another principle which has to do with lines in a costume is called "opposition." This is a design in which the lines run nearly at right angles.

Exercise 24

Design a summer dress of voile, using 1-inch ruffles to represent the theme of opposition.

Exercise 25

Design a summer dress for a small child, the lines to represent the theme of opposition.

[39]

Tailored and Fancy Waist

CHAPTER IX

WAISTS

It would be difficult for us to imagine a statue of a Greek goddess in a shirt-waist and skirt. When the shirt-waist first came into vogue, there was great opposition to its use, and the prediction was made that the fashion would never be a lasting one. But we are at last resigned to the fact that the shirt-waist is here to stay. It has proved its use. The waist is practical, and the practical has often pushed aside the artistic. Therefore, we should be interested in making the waist as beautiful in its simplicity and appropriateness as possible.

On considering waists and their relation to costume design, it becomes necessary to consider the types of waists, the tailored waist and the fancy waist. The school girl is interested more in the tailored waist than in the fancy waist. For some time the fact has been established that the middy or sailor waist is the most popular separate waist for every-day wear for the school girl. And the thought that this fashion is distinctly American serves to accent its favor.

The tailored waist should follow the same principles of design used for the entire costume. That is, the waist should be suitable to the wearer and should be in harmony with the other parts of the costume. One idea should predominate, and that is, that the collar and cuffs may give the keynote of distinction to the waist, or the central idea may be left to the trimming.

In regard to materials, the first thought should be for the kind that launders easily. Plain materials are safest. Oftentimes a very small check is permissible, and many times stripes are in good taste; but unless the buyer has power to discriminate between good and poor designs, the best plan is to choose plain materials. Linen, pongee, and washable silks are the best materials for the school girl.

The fancy waist to be worn with the tailored suit requires even greater discrimination on the part of the designer. Naturally the first point to consider is the skirt with which it is to be worn. The waist must harmonize in color, and must be suitable in design to the material in the skirt. Many school girls would laugh at the idea of choosing a checked waist for a striped skirt, or a polka-dot waist for a checked skirt, and yet, every day many examples of similar combinations are to be seen.

There is a natural tendency among girls to buy an article simply because it is pretty, without regard to the relationship it must bear to the other parts of the costume. That is why we see pink waists worn with purple suits, and flowered waists worn with figured skirts.

In recent years thin materials have taken the place of the thick heavy materials formerly used for blouses. The thin materials lend themselves very adaptably to colored wool handwork, and a chance for very artistic results is possible. Time may be very profitably spent in the classroom, working out designs for waists of thin material to be embroidered in colored yarns, or dyed in batik effects.

No matter how attractively a waist may be made, it is well for the pupil to remember that whenever there is a choice, the one-piece dress should be selected in preference to the shirt-waist. It is more graceful, more artistic, and more becoming.

THE TAILORED WAIST
Exercise 26

After the outline of the waist has been drawn, following the directions in Exercise 1, the next step is the designing of the waist itself. Review the principles of balance, rhythm, and harmony in order to arrange more harmoniously the lines in waist design. Consider the balance of unequal spaces. Decide upon the dominant note or central idea. It may be buttons, tucks, or even collar and cuffs. As the designs made are individual, the stout girls in the class should be careful to avoid wide frills, ruffles and horizontal lines. Slim girls, on the other hand, should avoid too many vertical lines. The aim in designing a tailored waist should be for simplicity.

THE FANCY WAIST

In designing the fancy waist, use softer lines than those used in the tailored waist. Consider again what is to be the dominant idea in the waist, and lay the emphasis upon that. Avoid conflicting lines, and the "patch effect" which is the result of using too many tacked-on shapes. For the waist design, choose an appropriate one and apply it to the waist to be worked out in stitchery in the sewing class.

Exercise 27

Plan a design for a fancy waist to be worked out in wool stitchery. Design a batik blouse.

Skirt Showing Pockets

CHAPTER X

SKIRTS

The simplest way in which to study skirts is to class them according to the winter skirt or woolen skirt, and the summer or washable skirt. Each type of skirt follows practically the same principles of design. In designing the skirt, the first thing to remember is to make it full enough to allow freedom of movement. The lines of the skirt should harmonize with the lines of the figure. Tall, thin girls should avoid too many vertical lines in design, and stout girls should avoid too many horizontal lines.

Plaid and striped skirts have always been very popular with high school girls. But it must be remembered that they require very little or no trimming, and also that the colors of the plaids and stripes must be selected with care in order that they may harmonize with the other parts of the costume.

If one chooses to use pockets on a plain skirt, the fact should be kept in mind that the pockets are part of the skirt design and not bold patches of material tacked on without relation to the main lines of the skirt. In planning designs for skirts, special attention should be given to the shape and width of belts, for unimportant as this may seem, the beauty of the skirt often depends upon the belt.

Exercise 28

Design a skirt to be made of summer material, using pockets as part of the design. Draw the figure in India ink on a tan background and mount.

Exercise 29

Design a skirt to be made of woolen material, planning the design so that it will be suitable for a stout figure.

Exercise 30

Select a material from given samples, and draw a design for a skirt suitable to your own individual figure.

Note:—Make the drawings not smaller than four inches in length.

Tailored Suit

CHAPTER XI

COATS AND SUITS

Since the selection of coats, suits, and wraps depends upon the same principles which govern the choice of dresses, the problem here will be to plan suits best in design for the individual type. As to color, such as dark blue, brown and dark green are to be preferred to the lighter colors for everyday wear.

Exercise 31

Cut from a fashion sheet a suit which seems to express your own individuality. Mount on a suitable background.

Exercise 32

From an uncolored fashion sheet, cut out the picture of a winter coat. From another sheet cut out a hat to match, and color these to harmonize. If there is time, you might draw the designs for the hats and coats after your own ideas. Before doing so, however, refer to Chapter VI on "Art Principles."

CHAPTER XII

COLOR IN DRESS

So much has been written upon the theory of color, and the subject is such an exhaustive one, that the space allotted here necessitates putting a few rules of "color as applied to dress design" in a very simple form.

By the time a girl reaches high school, she has a fair knowledge of the primary and secondary colors, and their relation to each other in the spectrum. She is still at a loss, however, to know how to combine colors successfully, and invariably hesitates when asked to choose suitable colors for her own particular type.

We know that from red, yellow, and blue, all other colors are made. For the purpose of placing color harmony in a systematic form, we shall consider, first of all, complementary colors.

Complementary colors are those that stand opposite to each other on the color wheel and enrich each other when placed together. The three pairs of complementary colors are: red and green, blue and orange, and yellow and violet. More interest in color harmony is aroused among the students if they are led to look for these different color harmonies in nature.

For the first pair of complementary colors, this harmony is repeated in the geranium, tulip, holly, clover, cherries, watermelon, and in many other flowers and vegetables. For the second pair, the violet, forget-me-not, clematis, and the blue plum show this relation. For the third pair, the wild aster, pansy, lilac, and the sky at sunset— pale violet clouds against a background of brilliant yellow. Nature blends the color harmonies with rich and beautiful effects, and the search for these examples leads to discrimination in color.

CHAPTER XIII

COLOR HARMONY

The simplest harmony is dominant harmony. This is a harmony of two or more tones of one color, or a harmony in which one color prevades throughout, such as tints and shades of brown, tints and shades of green. More examples of this relation of color are found in nature than any other combination.

Analogous harmony is a harmony of two or more colors very much alike in some respects, but differing in others. This harmony is based upon a contrast of values. In the color circle of thirteen, a better way to remember analogous colors is to select those colors which are adjoining. Examples of analogous harmonies are: Red, red-orange, and orange; or red, red-violet, and violet.

A contrasting harmony is a combination of two colors which are different in hue and value and which require a third color to bring them into harmony. Owing to the skill required to obtain an effective result in the combination of these apparently opposite colors, the pupils will find this harmcny probably the most difficult to master. Examples: Sage-green, cream, rose and black; or gray-blue, black or gold; gray-blue, red with black or gold.

CHAPTER XIV

COLOR HARMONY APPLIED TO DRESS

The following suggestions will be found helpful to the pupils:

1. Colors should not be widely separated in value.

2. Brilliant colors should be used only in small quantities.

3. Decide upon the dominant note of color in the costume, and bring the other colors into close harmonious relation to it.

4. A touch of black tends to bring colors closer together. With this purpose in mind, black is used by the very best designers.

5. For school costumes, where hats and shoes are also to be considered, dominant harmony is perhaps the most economical.

6. Care must be taken that the color chosen suits the type of the individual who is to wear it.

7. Girls with neutral coloring should wear pure colors.

8. Girls with pure coloring should wear neutral colors.

Exercise 33

Plan a color scheme in analogous harmony for some one in the class.

Exercise 34

Color two fashion plates, one in analogous harmony, and one in dominant harmony.

Trace three figures for a morning, an afternoon, and an evening dress, and color each appropriately. Mount the color schemes on suitable backgrounds.

CHARTS

If there is enough time in the course of costume design, the following charts may be made by the pupils:

1.   The six leading colors of the spectrum: red, yellow, orange, blue, green and violet.

2.   The intermediate colors, including red-orange, yellow-orange, yellow-green.

3.   The neutral colors: six hues of gray and brown.

4.   A chart of dominant harmony: blue, light blue, and dark blue.

5.   A chart of analogous harmony: blue, blue-violet, and red, red-violet.

6.   A chart of complementary harmony including the three pairs: red and green, blue and orange, yellow and violet.

7.   A chart of contrasting harmony; one color with a neutral.

Aside from this, the pupils should make color notes from memory, of flowers, fruits, and textiles.

CHAPTER XV

COLOR FOR DIFFERENT TYPES

Color, more than any other phase of costume design, makes or mars the personality of the wearer. It is almost impossible to classify each girl according to some special type and then dictate the colors she should wear. But every girl will be able to choose color schemes intelligently if she remembers that the color of her eyes, the color of her complexion, and the color of her hair give the keynote for the colors she should wear.

The fair blonde should wear light colors in preference to dark colors. One of her best colors is green. She may also wear successfully, tints of red, orange and blue. White she may wear, and also cream. Purple, above all other colors, should be avoided, and also yellow, brown and orange.

The pure blonde with a ruddy complexion has a problem all her own. She may wear colors of medium value; dark blue, green, and if her eyes are brown, she may wear tones of brown. Purple above all colors should be avoided.

The pale brunette should wear either light or dark colors and should avoid medium values. The colors that harmonize with her hair and eyes are the most becoming. She may successfully wear the following colors: Claret, deep reds, old rose, broken colors, like old gold. She must avoid, if she would be attractive, light and dark blue, olive green, gray and purple.

The brunette with a great deal of color looks best in pure color. Red, orange, vivid red, blue-green, scarlet, dark blue may be chosen. She must avoid light blue, very light green and purple, since purple is one of the most difficult colors to wear.

[52]

In regard to the "red" haired girl, browns which match the hue of the hair are the safest colors. She may also wear green in dull hues. Most "red" haired girls know by experiment that all tints and shades of red are to be avoided as well as colors that contain traces of yellow. Titian, who was fond of painting his "red" haired daughter, and who has given us many portraits of this interesting girl, found that certain hues of blue-green combined harmoniously with her type of beauty. The girl with "red" hair would do well to study the painting of Titian's daughter for examples of beautiful color schemes in costume. She will learn that pure colors are to be avoided if she would bring out her personality.

Too much cannot be said regarding the relations of complexions to color. Many pale-faced girls believe that by wearing very brilliant colors they counteract the paleness. The truth is that colors used this way in their fullest intensity only emphasize the paleness of the complexion. If one has a "yellow" complexion, this may be counteracted by wearing very light tan and natural color pongees. It is probably because of the freshness and whiteness of the skin, that children look best and fairest in white.

Just because a color is beautiful in itself is no reason why a girl should choose that color for her costume. A costume of broken orange on a girl of the dark brunette type adds life to the wearer, and adds a hundredfold to her personality. Whereas a dress made of the same material on a pale brunette detracts from her personality and makes the wearer positively uninteresting. Attractiveness becomes an effort instead of a result.

Purple is one of the most difficult colors to wear because it has a tendency to give the complexion a muddy appearance. Owing to its restfulness, mystery and symbolism, it is popular, but appropriate only in the gowns of older women. In most cases it looks entirely out of harmony when worn by a very young girl.

[53]

Sports Costume

CHAPTER XVI

SPORTS CLOTHES

American designers have copied draperies from the Greeks and dress lines from the French, but the sports costume has never been copied from any nation. Sports clothes are truly American. Foreign countries are now imitating American ideas in these clothes for outdoor wear.

The sports costume is distinctive. It is above all other things, dashing. Dashing in color and chic in design. Perhaps in no other designs do the various parts of the costume such as hats, wraps, and shoes blend so harmoniously as they do in the American clothes designed strictly for out-of-door wear.

The average sports costume consists of the sports skirt, the sports waist, usually covered by the sports coat, the hat, and the sports foot gear. If the skirt is made of vivid checked or striped material, the coat or sweater is plain in color, usually contrasting vividly. The hat matches in color either the coat or the skirt. Hats, with the exception of the stiff sailor, which is always in good taste, are usually made of soft material when planned for sports wear. There is sometimes a chance for hand work on the sports hat.

Exercise 35

Design a costume including a hat, short coat, skirt, blouse and shoes. Make the skirt of striped material and color the figure according to the suggestions given in this chapter.

Exercise 36

Design a sports costume, and color the entire outfit in harmony with a tan sports coat.

[55]

Hats for Different Types

CHAPTER XVII

HATS

One of the most important, as well as the most interesting phases of costume design is the study of hats and their relation to the individual types of girls.

In choosing a hat, the first consideration is given to the face, the second to its proportion in relation to the rest of the figure, and the third, its suitability to the costume with which it is to be worn. For convenience in the classroom, we consider first the three types of faces, the "oval," which requires a curved line in a hat; the "round" face, which requires a straight brim of the sailor type and not narrow; the "square" face, which requires a broken, irregular line.

The next step in the study of hats relates to the study of the individual profile. The chief factors to consider here are the nose and chin. The pupils should hold in mind two rules, that:

One who has a prominent nose should choose a hat with the trimming near the front, or on the front.

And, that one who has a projecting chin should choose a hat the trimming of which is behind the crown.

It is most important that a hat should not only suit the face, but also the figure. For this reason pupils should remember that:

(1) Small girls should avoid large drooping hats.

(2) Girls with very broad shoulders may counteract this by choosing a hat, the crown of which is fairly high and the brim broad.

(3) Very small hats should not be worn by people with large features. One must also have soft lines in the hair rather than severe lines in order to wear the small hat well.

(4) The large hat is usually considered the dress hat, and is becoming both to the large girl and to the tall, slender girl.

(5) Brilliant ornaments on the front of the hat should be avoided as they have a tendency to detract from the brilliancy of the eyes. In regard to color in hats, the same rules hold true that are true in color in costume designs.

(6) In choosing a hat, one should stand before a full length mirror in order to get the effect of the hat upon the proportion of the entire figure.

(7) School girls will do well to remember that the tailored hat is the most suitable for every day; and that gold lace, fancy feathers, and elaborate buckles should be avoided.

Exercise 37

Draw or cut from fashion magazines the three types of faces, the "oval," the "square," and the "round."

Illustrate the rule for each type by drawing a hat best suited for that particular type.

Illustrate the effect of choosing the wrong style of hat for each of the three types of faces.

Exercise 38

Draw a profile showing a prominent nose. Show the hat trimming near the front.

Draw a profile showing a projecting chin. In drawing the hat, place the trimming behind the crown.

Exercise 39

Sketch a humorous style of large drooping hat on a small figure.

Exercise 40

Cut from fashion magazines several distinct styles of hats, paste them across sheets of drawing paper, and print under each the type of face for which it is most suited.

Exercise 41

Cut a very tall figure from a fashion plate. Trace on drawing paper. Draw a hat on the figure with high vertical lines. Fill in with India ink. Make other humorous silhouettes.

CHAPTER XVIII

ACCESSORIES

A famous actress, noted throughout America for her artistic dress designs, once said, "An important detail in being well dressed is to be well groomed. A loose button, a missing hook, or a frayed edge spoils the entire appearance of one's gown. How often we have seen the damaging effect of soiled white gloves, or a pin replacing a missing button. Immaculate grooming and well-fitting garments, however moderate in cost they may be, look better by far than expensive materials which neither fit the person or the occasion, and show signs of the wearer's lack of heed for small details. Loose ends, spots, or makeshift pins in place of hooks ruin the entire ensemble however beautiful it may be in fabric or coloring."

She also says in regard to accessories: "If one must dress on a small allowance, it is always well to choose hats, gloves and shoes which are dark, and at the same time will look well with one's gowns and tailored garments."

What spectacles some students have made of themselves by appearing in public bedecked as an ancient Egyptian princess, who, not content with the shimmer of satins, arrayed herself in beads, armlets, anklets, necklaces, earrings, buckles and pectorals.

By accessories in costume we refer to gloves, shoes, stockings, handkerchiefs, pocket-books and jewelry.

Designs for Undergarments

CHAPTER XIX

UNDERGARMENTS
DESIGN
Exercise 42

Draw a number of geometric shapes, the square, the circle, the triangle, and the rectangle. Arrange groups for border designs. Plan a single design from the groups just drawn, giving special attention to the principles just learned.

Exercise 43

On a sheet of drawing paper 9 x 12 inches draw a square 2 x 2 inches, a rectangle 2 x 4 inches, and a circle 2½ inches in diameter. Use a leaf or flower shape as a motif and make three designs, giving special emphasis to harmony of line of the inclosed design to the outside shape.

A YOKE
Exercise 44

Fold a sheet of drawing paper 9 x 12 inches into two parts. Place a dot on the fold 3 inches from the top of the paper. From the dot draw a line to the right 3¼ inches long. Connect the line with a dot placed 3¼ inches to the right, across the top of the page. Cut on the lines. Fold a sheet of paper 7 x 3½ inches (the short way). From each side cut out a narrow strip. Open the pattern and trace the outline on the yoke, being careful to place the crease exactly in the center. When the outline has been traced, plan a series of tucks within the shape. Before attempting to arrange the tucks, a preliminary lesson on the review of the placing of parallel lines would be helpful.

Exercise 45

Cut a second yoke pattern following the directions in Exercise 44. Refer to Exercises 42 and 43 for suggestions for design. From a geometric shape plan a design suitable for an undergarment. Plan a second design from a natural motif. Following this lesson, plan a set of designs suitable for combination suits, nightgowns and other undergarments to be made in the sewing classes.

Exercise 46

When you have completed the yoke design on drawing paper, the best examples should be selected and traced on rice paper, and the design traced on thin paper with India ink.

Exercise 47

Draw four circles, each with a different diameter, the first one not larger than 1½ inches in diameter. Place a simple design in the center of the large circle and repeat the same design in the smaller circles. Draw a square 3 x 3 inches, and arrange the circles in the square to form a pleasing design. Fill the background spaces with harmonious shapes. Apply your designs to a paper pattern of the actual size of your own garment pattern.

CHAPTER XX

OUTLINE FOR STUDY OF HISTORY OF COSTUME

A reference to the history of the various periods of costume design will often throw an interesting light on the design of the costume itself. The personality of the rulers of the different periods of history is reflected in the costumes of that period. A study of the great masters of painting who enjoyed portraying the gentlemen and ladies of fashion is a very profitable pursuit in connection with costume design. The following outline is given merely for reference work:

Egyptian: Characterized by jeweled head-dress, ornamentation, elaborate embroidery, straight lines.

Greek: Beautiful in line and proportion. Mostly in draped effects.

Roman: In some ways an imitation of the Greek. The toga.

Byzantine: Richest of all periods in ornamentation and design. Jeweled silks.

Middle Ages: Very simple in style.

Medieval: Long cloaks and ornamented girdles. Hair dressed in long hanging braids.

Twelfth Century: The dress of the crusaders and monks.

Thirteenth Century: Same as the twelfth century. Heraldic decoration.

Fourteenth Century (Latter half): Tight garments used instead of the loosely flowing gowns.

Fifteenth Century (Early): Characterized by the exaggerated head-dress made usually over wire forms. More dignity.

Tudor Period (Early Sixteenth): Costly materials, long trains, large sleeves, girdles.

Sixteenth Century (The Renaissance): Full skirts, large sleeves, tight waist, high head-dress.

Elizabethan (Latter half of Sixteenth Century): High collars for men and women, much lace, wired skirts.

Louis Seize: Tight waist, short sleeves, short skirts.

Colonial (1770): See costumes of early American history.

Empire (1810): Very high waist line, very short puff sleeves, the scarf, long skirt, half bonnet.

Civil War Period (1860): Tight basque, long sleeve with cuff, long skirt, the bonnet.